Also by John Updike

FACING
NATURE

John Updike

FACING
NATURE

POEMS

Alfred A. Knopf · New York
1985

THIS IS A BORZOI BOOK
PUBLISHED BY ALFRED A. KNOPF, INC.

Published in the United States by Alfred A. Knopf, Inc.,
New York, and simultaneously in Canada by
Random House of Canada Limited, Toronto.
Distributed by Random House, Inc., New York.

Library of Congress Cataloging in Publication Data
Updike, John.
Facing nature.
I. Title.
PS3571.P4F3 1985   811'.54   84–48666
ISBN 0–394–54385–8

Manufactured in the United States of America
First Edition

ACKNOWLEDGMENTS

Some of these poems were previously published in *The New Republic*, *Harper's Magazine*, *The Atlantic*, *The American Scholar*, *The American Poetry Review*, *Ontario Review*, *The Saturday Review*, *The Bennington Review*, *The Connecticut Poetry Review*, *Plum*, *South Shore*, *The New York Quarterly*, *The New York Times*, *The Nation*, *Negative Capability*, *The Paris Review*, *Michigan Quarterly*, *New England Monthly*, and *Boston Magazine*. The following poems first appeared in *The New Yorker*: "Spanish Sonnets," "Energy: A Villanelle," "Penumbrae," "L.A.," "The Rockettes," "Aerie," "Gradations of Black," "The Furniture," "To Evaporation," and "To Crystallization." "Nature" originally appeared, with a Chinese translation, in *Modern Poetry: East and West* (Hong Kong: Shih Feng Association, 1981). "Plow Cemetery" was first published in *Antaeus*, 47, Autumn, 1982. "Long Shadow" first appeared in *Parabola*, 7, 1, 1983. "An Oddly Lovely Day Alone," "Iowa," "Small-City People," "Styles of Bloom" and "Two Sonnets Whose Titles Came to Me Simultaneously" were originally printed as broadsides by Waves Press (Richmond, Virginia), Press-22 (Portland, Oregon), Lord John Press (Northridge, California), and Palaemon Press (Winston-Salem, North Carolina) respectively. The small limited editions entitled *Sixteen Sonnets* (Halty Ferguson), *Five Poems* (Bits Press), and *Spring Trio* (Palaemon Press) all consisted of poems included in this volume. "Revelation" was written for the program of the Poets and Writers Celebration in New York City in October 1980.

CONTENTS

Sonnets

CONTENTS

Seven Odes to Seven Natural Processes

CONTENTS

Light Verse

Sonnets

TO ED SISSMAN

1.

I think a lot about you, Ed:
tell me why. Your sallow owlish face
with the gray wart where death had kissed it,
drifting sideways above your second gin
in Joseph's, at lunch, where with a what-the-hell
lurch you had commanded the waiter
to bring more poison, hangs in my mind
as a bloated star I wish to be brave on.

I loved your stuff, and the way
it came from nowhere, where poetry
must come from, having no credentials.
Your talk was bland, with a twist of whine,
of the obvious man affronted. You stooped
more and more, shouldering the dark for me.

II.

When you left, the ceiling caved in.
The impossible shrank to the plausible.
In that final room, where one last book
to be reviewed sat on your chest, you said,
like an incubus, transparent tubes
moved in and out of your veins
and nurses with volleyball breasts
mocked us with cheerleader health.

You were sicker than I, but I huddled in
my divorcing man's raincoat by your bed
like a drenched detective by the cozy fire
a genial suspect has laid in his manor,
unsuspecting he is scheduled Next Victim.
I mourned I could not solve the mystery.

III.

You told me, lunching at Josèph's,
foreseeing death, that it would be
a comfort to believe. My faith,
a kind of rabbit frozen in the headlights,
scrambled for cover in the roadside brush
of gossip; your burning beams passed by.
"Receiving communications from beyond": thus
you once described the fit of writing well

The hint hangs undeveloped, like
my mental note to send you Kierkegaard.
Forgive me, Ed; no preacher, I—
a lover of the dust, like you,
who took ten years of life on trial
and gave pentameter another voice.

WAITING ROOMS

Boston Lying-In

Here women, frightened, bring their sex
as black men bring their wounds to the nighttown ward,
red evidence of rampages they ask
abstracted doctors to forgive,
forgive and understand and heal.
That snubnose has a secret in her crotch;
she holds some kind of order slip, a clue
in triplicate, at a loss for the proper desk.

They will bleed her and splay her and bed her
in sheets too white, in a bed too narrow;
black women will tend her sardonically
while men with hands scrubbed too often will peer
into the heart of anfractuous love.
Our bottoms betray us and beg for the light.

Mass. Mental Health

The mad are mad for cigarettes;
slightly shouting in their brain-deaf way,
they bum from one another with angry eyes
that run on separate circuits from their mouths.
The men, a-twitch, in curious rags
of their own combining, seem to have shaved
at some half-lit hour when nothing counted.
Glowering, knotted, their brows are shamed.

The women are different—haughty tramps
exhaling. One wears a paper hat
and has good legs, though bitten nails.
She asks me, "You a doctor?" I say, "No,"
all agitated. When men crack, we expect
murder to out; when women crack, sex.

TWO SONNETS WHOSE TITLES CAME TO ME SIMULTANEOUSLY

The Dying Phobiac Takes His Fears with Him

Visions of flame fanned out from cigarette
or insecure connection to engulf
all carpets, floors, and sleepers in their beds
torment no longer the shadow in his tent
of sterile plastic, his oblivious lungs
laboring to burn last oxygen,
his fear of heights dissolving as he hangs
high above hissing nothingness.

The dread of narrow places fails to visit
his claustral tent, and hydrophobia,
amid the confluence of apparatus,
runs swirling down a drain. His nerves and veins
release their fibrous demons; earth and air
annul their old contract and set him free.

No More Access to Her Underpants

Her red dress stretched across the remembered small
of her dear bare back, bare for me no more,
that once so softly bent itself in bed
to take my thrusts and then my stunned caress,
disclosing to my sated gaze a film
of down, of sheen, upon the dulcet skin—
her red dress stretched, I say, as carapace
upon her tasty flesh, she shows a face

of stone and turns to others at the party.
Her ass, its solemn cleft; her breasts, their tips
as tender in color as the milk-white bit
above the pubic curls; her eyes like pits
of warmth in the tousled light: all forfeit,
and locked in antarctic ice by this bitch.

UPON THE LAST DAY
OF HIS FORTY-NINTH YEAR

Scritch, scratch, saith the frozen spring snow—
not near enough this season or the last,
but still a skin for skiing on, with care.
At every shaky turn into the fall line
one hundred eighty pounds of tired blood
and innards weakly laced with muscle seek
to give themselves to gravity and ruin.
My knees, a-tremble with old reflex, resist

and try to find the lazy dancer's step
and pillowed curve my edges flirted with
when I had little children to amaze
and life seemed endlessly flexible. Now,
my heavy body swings to face the valley
and feels the gut pull of steep maturity.

LONG SHADOW

Crossing from a chore as the day
was packing it in, I saw my long shadow
walking before me, bearing in the tilt
of its thin head autumnal news,
news broadcast red from the woods to the west,
the goldleaf woods of shedding branch and days
drawing in like a purse being cinched,
the wintry houses sealed and welcoming.

Why do we love them, these last days of something
like summer, of freedom to move in few clothes,
though frost has flattened the morning grass?
They tell us we shall live forever. Stretched
like a rainbow across day's end, my shadow
makes a path from my feet; I am my path.

L.A.

Lo, at its center one can find oneself
atop a paved and windy hill, with weeds
taller than men on one side and on the other
a freeway thundering a canyon's depth below.
New buildings in all mirror-styles of blankness
are being assembled by darkish people while
the tan-bricked business blocks that Harold Lloyd
teetered upon crouch low, in shade, turned slum.

The lone pedestrian stares, scooped at by space.
The palms are isolate, like psychopaths.
Conquistadorial fevers reminisce
in the adobe band of smog across the sky,
its bell of blue a promise that lured too many
to this waste of angels, of ever-widening gaps.

RICHMOND

The shadows in his eye sockets like shades
upon a bearded hippie, Stonewall Jackson
stares down Monument Avenue toward where Lee
sits on an even higher horse. The cause
was lost but lingers in the subtly defiant
dignity of the pale-gray, Doric dollhouse
wherefrom Jeff Davis, conscientious Satan,
directed our second rebellion: a damn good try.

Brick graciousness prevails; across the James
wood houses hold black pensioners, and Poe's
ghost haunts a set of scattered tombs, *musei*
exposing to Northern visitors his quills,
a model of his muddy city, and
an etching of, wry-necked in death, Virginia.

OHIO

1.

Rolling along through Ohio,
lapping up Mozart on the radio
(Piano
Concerto No. 21, worn but pure),
having awoken while dawn
was muddying a rainy sky,
I learned what human was:
human was the music,

natural was the static
blotting out an arpeggio
with clouds of idiot rage,
exploding, barking, blind.
The stars sit athwart our thoughts
just so.

11.

To be fair, though, about that day—
dull sky, scuds of goldenrod,
fields dried flat, the plain hinting
at a tornado,
the choleric sun
a pillowed sort of face upon
which an antic wisp of cirrus
had set a mustache—

at dawn, I remembered all day,
I had parked beneath an overpass
to check my lights, and breathed
the secret green, the rain.
Like hammered melody the empty road
soared east and west. No static. Air.

IOWA

White barns this morning match the trees
whitewashed by fog that tiptoed in
among the little hills and froze.
Was all land once so innocent?
Did all our country uncles come to rest
on such long porches fortified
by moats of lawn where fireflies and dew
compounded the smoke of their summer cigars?

Those fireflies! From gloomy aisles of corn,
from lakeside groves the lanterns come.
This winter holds them in it like a jar—
contours of ripeness cast in frost
like old lawn furniture of iron,
our fruited plain as virgin as the moon.

SPANISH SONNETS

for Martha

1.

By the light of insomnia, truths
that by daylight don't look so bad—
one is over the hill, will die, and has
an appointment tomorrow that can't be broken—
become a set of slippery caves.
Bare facts that cast no shadow at noon
echo and shudder, swallow and loom.
To be alive is to be mad.

Can it be? Only Goya pictures it.
Those last brown paintings smeared in Madrid
fill a room with insomnia's visions,
a Spanish language rapid as a curse.
Prayer's a joke, love a secretion;
the tortured torture, and worse gets worse.

11.

He omits, Goya, not even the good news:
the pink-cheeked peasants in the ideal open,
the village health, the ring of children,
in days when everyone dressed like lords.
Carlos the Fourth wears a fool's mild smile,
and the royal family, a row of breeders,
are softly human, and in this style still
the white-shirted rebel throws up his arms.

The red scream darkens, the brushstrokes plunge
headlong into Rouault, where evil
faces are framed like saints' by lead.
The astonishing *Half-Hidden Dog*
for a sky has a Turner. Pain is paint
and people are meat, as for Francis Bacon.

III.

Yes, self-obsession fills our daily clothes,
bulges them outward like armor,
but at night self must be shed,
the room must be hollow, each lamp
and table crazily exact, and the door
snug in the frame of its silence. When we
can imagine the room when we are not there,
we are asleep. The world hasn't ended.

I worry for you a hemisphere away,
awaiting the edge of evening while I,
deep in midnight, plump the pillow,
turn on the light, and curse the clock.
The planet's giant motion overpowers us.
We cannot stop clinging where we are.

IV.

Each day's tour, I gather sandy castles,
cathedrals of marzipan gone bad,
baroque exploding sunbursts in Toledo,
filigreed silver crosses in Ávila,
like magnified mold proliferating.
The tragical stink of old religion—
greasy-eyed painters trying too hard,
crucifix-carvers gone black in the thumb.

And the Moor piled up brick and ochre,
and the Christian nailed iron in turn
to the gates of the city, and the land breathes green
under power lines hung upon windmills,
and I try to picture your body part by part
to supplant the day's crenellated loot.

V.

The land is dry enough to make the rivers
dramatic here. You say you love me;
as the answer to your thirst, I splash,
fall, and flow, a varied cool color.
Here fountains celebrate intersections,
and our little Fiats eddy and whirl
on the way to siesta and back.
They say don't drink tap water, but I do.

Unable to sleep, I make water at night
to lighten myself for a phantom trip.
My image in the mirror is undramatic,
merely old and nude—a wineskin.
Who could ever love me? Misread
road maps pour out of me in a stream.

VI.

Neumático punturado—we stopped
on the only empty spot in Spain,
a concrete stub road forgotten between
a steep grass slope up to an orange wall
and a froth of mustard veiling two poppies.
Blessedly, the native space held back,
the Fiat held mute while we puzzled through
its code of metal to the spare and the jack.

¡Milagro! It rose like a saint, the car,
on a stiff sunbeam; nuts fell from the wheel
with the ease of bread breaking. The change
achieved, we thankfully looked up. Three men
in sky-blue work clothes in a sky of green
silently wielded sickles. They had seen.

VII.

All crises pass, though not the condition of crisis.
Today I saw Franco as a bookend, with Juan Carlos.
The king is much on television, and indeed
seems telegenic. Slept well last night,
with dreams in deeper colors than there are.
Imagine a cardinal's biscuit palace, friable,
from whose uncountable windows peep
hospital bedsteads painted lime green:

I saw this in sunlight. The people
are clean, white, courteous, industrious.
To buy an inner tube, pay a traffic fine,
order Cinzano—this is civilization.
The streets, though dim, are safe at night. Lovers
touch, widows wear black, all is known.

VIII.

These islands of history amid traffic snarls—
Joanna the Mad in Tordesillas
played the harpsichord, leaned on the parapet,
saw a river, great fields, a single man
hooking a sheep who had gone the wrong way;
in Valladolid, Álvaro de Luna
knelt in the tiny, now dirty plaqued plaza
called Ochavo to be beheaded.

These souls thought the stars heaved with them.
My life has seamed shut; I sleep
as return to you dawns like a comet.
Rubber tires burn where martyrs bled,
the madness of sunshine melts the plain,
tulips outnumber truths in my Madrid.

Poems

SPRING SONG

The fiddlehead ferns down by our pond
stand like the stems of violins
the worms are playing beneath the moss.

Last autumn's leaves are pierced by shoots
that turn from sickly-pale to green.
All growth's a slave, and rot is boss.

STYLES OF BLOOM

One sudden week (the roads still salty,
and only garlic green) forsythia
shouts out in butter-yellow monotone
from hedge to hedge and yard to yard,
a shout the ochre that precedes
maple leaves echoes overhead.

The dogwood's blossoms float sideways
like stars in the dark that teatime brings
to the side of the tall brick house,
but almost vanish, melting flakes,
in morning's bald spring sun.

Lilac: an explosion of ego
odorous creamily, each raceme
dewy till noon, and then overnight
papery and faded—a souvenir.

In arches weighed by fragile suds,
the bridal wreath looks drenched.
White as virtue is white, plain
as truth is plain, the bushes can't wait
to shed their fat bundles of sequins.
Burdensome summer has come.

NATURAL QUESTION

What rich joke does
the comically spherical peony bud—
like the big button on a gong striker—
hold, that black ants
crawl all over its tie-dyed tightness,
as if to tickle it forth?

ACCUMULATION

Busbound out of New York
through New Jersey,
one sees a mountain of trash,
a hill of inhuman dimension, with trucks
filing up its slopes like ants
and filing down empty, back to the city
for more.
Green plastic flutters from the mountain's sides
and flattened tin glints through the fill
that bulldozer treads have tamped
in swatches like enormous cloth.
One wonders, does it have a name,
this hill,
and has any top been set
to its garbagy growing?

Miles pass.
A cut by the side of the eight-
lane concrete highway
(where spun rubber and dripped oil
accumulate)
has exposed a great gesture of shale—
sediment hardened, coarse page by page,
then broken and swirled like running water,
then tipped and infolded by time,
and now cut open like a pattern of wood
when grain is splayed to make a butterfly.
Gray aeons stand exposed in this gesture,
this half-unfurling

on the way to a fuller unfurling
wherein our lives will have been of less moment
than grains of sand tumbled back and forth
by the solidifying tides.

Our past
lies at the end of this journey.
The days bringing each their detritus,
the years minute by minute have lifted
us free of our home,
that muck whose every particle—
the sidewalk cracks, the gravel alleys—
we hugged to our minds as matrix,
a cozy ooze.
What mountains we are,
all impalpable, and
perishable as tissue
crumpled into a ball and tossed upon the flames!
Lives, lives.
The faces outside the bus window
have the doughy, stoic look of those
who grew up where I did,
ages ago.

PLOW CEMETERY

The Plow: one of the three-mile inns that nicked
the roads that led to Reading and eased the way.
From this, Plow Hill, Plowville—a little herd
of sandstone, barn and house like cow and calf,
brown-sided—and, atop the hill, Plow Church,
a lumpy Lutheran pride whose bellied stones
Grandfather Hoyer as a young buck wheeled
in a clumsy barrow up the bending planks
that scaffolded around the rising spire.
He never did forget how those planks bent
beneath his weight conjoined with that of rock,
on high; he would tell of it in the tone
with which he recounted, to childish me,
dental pain he had endured. The drill,
the dentist warned him, would approach the nerve.
"And indeed it did approach it, very close!"
he said, with satisfaction, savoring
the epic taste his past had in his mouth.

What a view he must have commanded then,
the hickory handles tugging in his palms!—
the blue-green hills, Reading a vast brick smudge
eleven winding miles away. The northward view
is spacious even from the cemetery,
Plow Cemetery, downhill from the church.
Here rest my maternal forebears underneath
erect or slightly tipping slender stones,
the earliest inscribed *Hier ruhe*, then
with arcs of sentimental English set

afloat above the still-Germanic names
in round relief the regional soft rock
releases to the air slow grain by grain
until the dates that framed a brisk existence
spent stamping amid animals and weather
are weathered into timelessness. Still sharp,
however, V-cut in imported granite,
stand shadowed forth John Hoyer's name, his wife's,
his daughter's, and his son-in-law's. All four
mar one slab as in life they filled one house,
my mother's final year left blank. Alert
and busy aboveground, she's bought a plot
for me, for *me*, in Plow Cemetery.

Our earth here is red, like blood mixed with flour,
and slices easy; my cousin could dig
a grave in a morning with pick and shovel.
Now his son, also my cousin, mounts
a backhoe, and the shuddering machine
quick-piles what undertakers, for the service,
cloak in artificial turf as tinny
as Christmas. New mounds weep pink in the rain.
Live moles tummock the porous, grassy ground.
Traffic along Route 10 is quieter now
the Interstate exists in parallel,
forming a four-lane S in the middle view
that wasn't there before, this side the smudge
red Reading makes between its blue-brown hills.
Except for this and ever-fresher graves,
all changes are organic here. At first,
I did resent my mother's heavy gift,
her plot to bring me home; but slowly I

have come to think, Why not? Where else? I will
have been away for fifty years, perhaps,
but have forever to make my absence up.
My life in time will seal shut like a scar.

NATURE

is such a touching child.
When his first wife and he
had their tennis court built,
they were going to plant cedars
(transplanted from the field)
all around it, to make
a windscreen.
The digging proved hard,
the wheelbarrow awkward,
and they planted only one,
at the corner.
Now, years later, returning
to drop off a child,
he sees the forgotten cedar
has grown tall enough
to be part of a windscreen
if there were others with it,
if it had not grown alone.

PLANTING TREES

Our last connection with the mythic.
My mother remembers the day as a girl
she jumped across a little spruce
that now overtops the sandstone house
where still she lives; her face delights
at the thought of her years translated
into wood so tall, into so mighty
a peer of the birds and the wind.

Too, the old farmer still stout of step
treads through the orchard he has outlasted
but for some hollow-trunked much-lopped
apples and Bartlett pears. The dogwood
planted to mark my birth flowers each April,
a soundless explosion. We tell its story
time after time: the drizzling day,
the fragile sapling that had to be staked.

At the back of our acre here, my wife and I,
freshly moved in, freshly together,
transplanted two hemlocks that guarded our door
gloomily, green gnomes a meter high.
One died, gray as a sagebrush next spring.
The other lives on and some day will dominate
this view no longer mine, its great
lazy feathery hemlock limbs down-drooping,
its tent-shaped caverns resinous and deep.
Then may I return, an old man, a trespasser,

and remember and marvel to see
my small deeds, that hurried day, with my wife,
so amplified, like a story through layers of air
told over and over, spreading.

PENUMBRAE

The shadows have their seasons, too.
The feathery web the budding maples
cast down upon the sullen lawn

bears but a faint relation to
high summer's umbrageous weight
and tunnellike continuum—

black leached from green, deep pools
wherein a globe of gnats revolves
as airy as an astrolabe.

The thinning shade of autumn is
an inherited Oriental,
red worn to pink, nap worn to thread.

Shadows on snow look blue. The skier,
exultant at the summit, sees his poles
elongate toward the valley: thus

each blade of grass projects another
opposite the sun, and in marshes
the mesh is infinite,

as the winged eclipse an eagle in flight
drags across the desert floor
is infinitesimal.

And shadows on water!—
the beech bough bent to the speckled lake
where silt motes flicker gold,

or the steel dock underslung
with a submarine that trembles,
its ladder stiffened by air.

And loveliest, because least looked-for,
gray on gray, the stripes
the pearl-white winter sun

hung low beneath the leafless wood
draws out from trunk to trunk across the road
like a stairway that does not rise.

THE CODE

Were there no rain there would be little noise,
no rustle on the roof that we confuse
with our own bloodbeat on the inner ear,
no braided gurgle in the gutter, no breathing
within the tree whose shelved and folded bulk
sifts the rain to a mist of small descents.

A visitor come from a cloudless planet
would stand amazed by the tumults of our water
and feel bereaved. Without the rain
the taxi wheels would pass like wind on sand
and all the splashing that excites our lovers
fresh from drinks would be a chastening calm;

the sky would be devoid of those enormous
companions who hang invisible
until our wish to see brings forth in focus
their sliding incandescent shapes.
Without the rain the very links of life
would drift still uncemented, a dream of dust.

Were there no rain the windowpanes
would never tick as if a spy outside,
who once conspired with us to ferret out
the secret code, the terms of full concord
with all that is and will be, were signalling
with a fingernail, *I'm back, I've got the goods*.

REVELATION

Two days with one eye:
doctor said I had to wear a patch
to ward off infection
in the abraded cornea.

As hard to get used to as the dark:
no third dimension
and the swaddled eye
reporting a gauze blur to the brain.

You feel clumsy:
hearing and thinking affected also.
Only your sense of smell improves
in a world of foggy card-shapes.

When the patch came off on Monday,
the real world was alarming,
bulging every which way and bright:
a kind of a joke, a pop-up book.

SLEEPING WITH YOU

One creature, not the mollusk
clamped around an orgasm, but
more loosely biune, we are linked
by tugs of the blanket and dreams whose disquiet
trembles to the other body, creating
those eddies of semi-wakefulness wherein
we acknowledge the other is there
as an arm is there, or an ancestor,
or any fact admitted yet not known.

What body is warm beside mine,
what corpse has been slain
on this soft battlefield where we wounded
lift our heads to cry for water
or to ask what forces prevailed?
It is you, not dead, but entrusted
at my side to the flight the chemical mind
must take or be crazed, leaving the body
behind like matériel in a trench.

The moon throws back sunlight into the woods,
but whiter, cleansed by its bounce
amid the cold stars, and the owls
fly their unthinkable paths to pluck
the bleached shrew from her bed of leaves.
Dreaming rotates us, but fear
leads us to cling each to each as a spar
is clung to by the shipwrecked
till dawn brings sky-fire and rescue.

Your breathing, relaxed to its center,
scrapes like a stone on rough fiber,
over and over. Your skin, steeped
in its forgetting, sweats,
and flurries of footwork bring you near
the surface; but then your rapt lungs slip
with a sigh back into the healing,
that unpoliced swirling of spirit
whose sharing is a synonym for love.

AN ODDLY LOVELY DAY ALONE

The kids went off to school,
the wife to the hairdresser,
or so she said, in Boston—
"He takes forever. 'Bye."

I read a book, doing my job.
Around eleven, the rat man came—
our man from Pest Control,
though our rats have long since died.

He wears his hair rat-style—
cut short, brushed back—and told me
his minister had written a book
and "went on television with it."

The proceeds, however, unlike mine,
would be devoted, every cent,
to a missionary church
in Yucatán.

Time went by silently. For lunch,
I warmed up last night's pizza,
and added my plate to the dishwasher,
and soap, and punched FULL CYCLE.

A book, a box of raisins,
and bed. The phone rang once,
a woman whose grant had not come through,
no fault of mine.

"That's all right," I told her.
"Just yesterday,
I failed to win
the National Book Critics' Circle Prize."

The book was good. The bed was warm.
Each hour seemed a rubber band
the preoccupied fingers of God
were stretching at His desk.

A thump, not a dishwasher thump.
The afternoon paper: it said
an earthquake had struck Iran
mere minutes after the Shah had left.

The moral seemed clear.
More time passed, darkening.
All suddenly unbeknownst,
the afternoon had begun to snow—

to darken, darken and snow:
a fantastic effect, widespread.
If people don't entertain you,
Nature will.

SMALL-CITY PEOPLE

They look shabby and crazy but not
in the campy big-city way of those
who really would kill you or really do
have a million dollars in the safe at home—
dudes of the absolute, swells of the dark.

Small-city people hardly expect to get
looked at, in their parkas
and their hunting caps and babushkas
and Dacron suits and outmoded
bouffants. No tourists come
to town to stare, no Japanese
or roving photographers.

The great empty mills, the wide main drag
with its boarded-up display windows,
the clouded skies that never quite rain
form a rock there is no out from under.

The girls look tough, the men look tired,
the old people dress up for a circus called off
because of soot, and snarl
with halfhearted fury, their hats
on backwards. The genetic pool
confluxes to cast up a rare beauty,
or a boy full of brains:
these can languish as in a desert
or eventually flourish, for not being
exploited too soon.

Small cities are kind, for
failure is everywhere, ungrudging;
not to mention free parking
and bowls of little pretzels in the ethnic bars.
Small-city people know what they know,
and what they know is what you learn
only living in a place
no one would choose but that chose you,
flatteringly.

THE FLECKINGS

The way our American wildflowers hover
　　and spatter and fleck the underlying ground
was understood the best by Winslow Homer;

with brush and palette knife he marred the somber
　　foreground field of the mountainous *Two Guides*
and slashed the carpet green of *Boys in a Pasture*.

So all our art; these casual stabs of color—
　　Abstract Expressionism ere it had a name—
proclaim the violence underfoot discovered.

TWO HOPPERS

Displayed in the Thyssen-Bornemisza Collection

The smaller, older *Girl at a Sewing Machine*
    shows her, pale profile obscured by her hair,
at work beneath an orange wall while sky

in pure blue pillars stands in a window bay.
    She is alone and silent. The heroine
of *Hotel Room*, down to her slip, gazes

at a letter unfolded upon her naked knees.
    Her eyes and face are in shadow. The day
rumbles with invisible traffic outside

this room where a wall is yellow, where
    a bureau blocks our way with brown and luggage
stands in wait of its unpacking near

a green armchair: sun-wearied, Thirties plush.
    We have been here before. The slanting light,
the woman alone and held amid the planes

of paint by some mysterious witness we're
    invited to breathe beside. The sewing girl,
the letter. Hopper is saying, *I am Vermeer.*

GRADATIONS OF BLACK

(Third Floor, Whitney Museum)

Ad Reinhardt's black, in *Abstract Painting 33*,
　　seems atmosphere, leading the eye into
that darkness where, self-awakened, we

grope for the bathroom switch; no light goes on,
　　but we come to see that the corners of his square
black canvas are squares slightly, slightly brown.

Frank Stella, in *Die Fahne Hoch*, aligns
　　right-angled stripes, dark gray, upon black ground
lustrous and granular like the magnified

skin of a tattooed Nigerian slave.
　　The black of Mark Rothko's *Four Darks in Red*
holds grief; small lakes of sheen ebb away,

and the eye, seeking to sink, is rebuffed
　　by a much-worked dullness, the patina of a rag
that oily Vulcan uses, wiping up.

While Clyfford Still, in his tall *Untitled*,
　　has laid on black in flakes of hardening tar,
a dragon's scales so slick the viewer's head

is mirrored, a murky helmet, as he stands
　　waiting for the flame-shaped passion to clear.
With broad house-painter's brush and sweeping hands

Franz Kline, in *Mahoning*, barred radiance; now each
    black gobby girder has yielded cracks to time
and lets leak through the dead white underneath.

HEAD OF A GIRL, AT THE MET

Vermeer's girl in your turban and pearl:
I saw you once in The Hague, some sixteen years ago,
and now in New York as part of this visiting show.
   You haven't changed, you famous girl,

   your lower lip as moist and thoughtful
as the painter's touch could render it, your eyes
resting sideways on mine, their gaze weighted by
   that fullness of a woman's eyeball.

   I, I have changed a great deal:
hair brown then now gray, heart fresh as red paint
veined now by the crackling of too many days
   hung in the harsh sun of the real.

   You will outlive me, artful girl,
and with averted head will rest your moment's glance
on centuries of devotees (barring mischance),
   the light in your eyes like the light on your pearl.

THE FURNITURE

To things we are ghosts, soft shapes
in their blindness that push and pull,
a warm touch tugging on a stuck drawer,
a face glancing by in a mirror
like a pebble skipped across a passive pond.

They hear rumors of us, things, in their own rumble,
and notice they are not where they were in the last
        century,
and feel, perhaps, themselves lifted by tides
of desire, of coveting; a certain moisture
mildews their surfaces, and they guess that we have
        passed.

They decay, of course, but so slowly; a vase
or mug survives a thousand uses. Our successive
ownerships slip from them, our fury
flickers at their reverie's dimmest edge.
Their numb solidity sleeps through our screams.

Those photographs Victorian travellers
produced of tombs and temples still intact
contain, sometimes, a camel driver, or beggar: a brown
man in a gallabiyah who moved his head, his life
a blur, a dark smear on the unchanging stone.

PAIN

flattens the world—its bubbles
of bliss, its epiphanies, the upright
sticks of day-to-day business—
and shows us what seriousness is.

And shows us, too, how those around us
do not and cannot share
our being; though men talk animatedly
and challenge silence with laughter

and women bring their engendering smiles
and eyes of famous mercy,
these kind things slide away
like rain beating on a filthy window

when pain interposes.
What children's pageant in gauze
filled the skull's ballroom before
the caped dark stranger commanded, *Freeze*?

Life is worse than folly. We live
within a cage wherefrom escape
annihilates the captive; this, too,
pain leads us to consider anew.

TASTE

I have, alas, no taste—
taste, that Talleyrand, that ally of the minimal,
that foreign-accented intuiter
of what sly harmonies exist
betwixt the draped, the draper, and the drape:
that advocate of the *right* as it teeters
on its tightrope above the abyss of excess,
beneath the airy tent-top of not quite enough.

My first wife had taste.
White walls were her answer, and, Take that
to the attic. Nothing pleased her, quite,
but Cézanne and emptiness
and a shabby Oriental rug so full
of dust and virtue it made me sneeze,
descended as it was from her ancestors,
exemplary in piety and in the China trade.
Yet she was *right*, right in all things,
and draped herself in cocktail dresses
of utter black, her arms no less perfect than bones.

I know a man with taste.
He lives alone on a floor of a warehouse
and designs machines that make nothing
but vivid impressions of whirling,
of ellipticity, dazzle, and flow.
He cooks on a single burner
Suprêmes de Volaille aux Champignons,

has hung his brick walls with pencilled originals
by Impressionist masters,
and lives in smiling harmony with all that is there
and is not there,
minding only the traffic noise from the street.
He and my first wife would make a pair,
but they will never meet.

My second wife, that flatterer, says
I have taste.
All decisions as to pattern are deferred to me.
A chair, a car I chose is cheered
when it arrives, like a bugle note, on pitch
with all the still-humming chords
of our clamorous, congratulatory mingling.
It makes one blush, to be credited with taste.
Chipmunk fur, wave-patterns on sand, white asters—
but for these, and some few other exceptions,
Nature has no taste, just productivity.
I want to be, like Nature, tasteless,
abundant, reckless, cheerful. Go screw, taste—
itself a tasteless suggestion.

ANOTHER DOG'S DEATH

For days the good old bitch had been dying, her back
pinched down to the spine and arched to ease the pain,
   her kidneys dry, her muzzle gray. At last
I took a shovel into the woods and dug her grave

In preparation for the certain. She came along,
which I had not expected. Still, the children gone,
   such expeditions were rare, and the dog,
spayed early, knew no nonhuman word for love.

So she made her stiff legs trot and let her bent tail wag.
We found a spot we liked, where the pines met the field.
   The sun warmed her fur as she dozed and I dug;
I carved her a safe place while she guarded me.

I measured her length with the shovel's handle;
she perked in amusement, and sniffed the heaped earth.
   Back down at the house, she seemed friskier,
but gagged, eating. We called the vet a few days later.

They were old friends. She held up a paw, and he
injected a violet fluid. She swooned on the lawn,
   and we watched her breathing slowly ebb to naught.
In the wheelbarrow up to the hole, her fur took the sun.

CRAB CRACK

for Michael and Mary Jane

*In the
Pond*
The blue crabs come to the brown pond's edge
to browse for food where the shallows are warm
and small life thrives subaqueously,
while we approach from the airy side,
great creatures bred in trees and armed
with nets on poles of such a length
as to outreach that sideways tiptoe lurch
when, in a dark splash from above, the crabs
discover themselves to be prey.

                           We can feel
at the pole's other end their fearful

*In the
Bucket*
wide-legged kicking, like the fury of scissors
if scissors had muscle. We want
their sweet muscle. Blue and a multitude
of colors less easily named (scum green,
old ivory, odd ovals of lipstick red
where the blue-glazed limbs are hinged),
they rest in the buckets, gripping one another
feebly, like old men fumbling in their laps,
numb with puzzlement, their brains
a few threads, each face a mere notch
on the brittle bloated pancake of the carapace.

*In the
Pot*
But the passion with which they resist!
Even out of the boiling pot they come clattering
and try to dig holes in the slick kitchen floor
and flee as if hours parching in the sun
on the lawn beneath our loud cocktails
had not taught them a particle of despair.

On the
Table
Now they are done, red. Cracking
their preposterous backs, we cannot bear
to touch the tender fossils of their mouths
and marvel at the beauty of the gills,
the sweetness of the swimmerets. All is exposed,
an intricate toy. Life spins such miracles
by multiples of millions, yet our hearts
never quite harden, never quite cease
to look for the hand of mercy in
such workmanship. If when we die, we're dead,
then the world is ours like gaudy grain
to be reaped while we're here, without guilt.
If not, then an ominous duty to feel
with the mite and the dragon is ours,
and a burden in being.

In the
Stomach
                              Late at night
the ghosts of the crabs patrol our intestines,
scampering sideways, hearkening *à pointe*
like radar dishes beneath the tide, seeking
the safe grave of sand in vain, turning,
against their burning wills, into us.

AERIE

By following many a color-coded corridor
and taking an elevator up through the heart of the hospital
amid patients with the indignant stare of parrots
from within their cages of drugs,
one can arrive at the barbershop
which the great institution keeps as a sop to the less-than-
    mortal needs
of its captive populace, its serried ranks of pain.

Here, a marvel: a tiny room, high above Boston,
lined with Polaroid photographs of happy, shorn cus-
    tomers,
and the barber himself asleep in two chairs,
snoring with the tranquillity of a mustached machine.
Nor is that all: opposite me,
not ten feet away from where I stood wondering what
    happened next,
a seagull on the ledge outside the windows with so
    dazzling a view
worried at the same problem. With his beak
he rapped at the glass. Once. Twice. Hard.

We two framed the problem, two sentient bookends
with slumber's fat volume between us.
The gull was accustomed to being fed stale breadcrusts,
    and the back
of my neck tickled unendurably, and the tops of my ears.
One man with an oblivious mustache between us held the
    answer

to both of our problems, but until he awoke
our gazes interlocked like the strengths of sumo wrestlers
     too caught up
in the effort of contention even to grunt.

And the sky swooped at the blue harbor and the great
     green steel bridge
trembled with its traffic, and the machines
keeping alive the terrified and comatose beneath us
     hummed
and the icons of old haircuts grinned in fading color
and all was as the earth is, poised in space between con-
     tending wishes,
until a sharper rap from the intelligent gull, or else
a more pointed clearing of my throat, awoke
the Demiurge, who, with not
a further wink, sized us up
and nimbly reached for his bag of old bread and his
     scissors.

THE SHUTTLE

Sitting airborne on the
New York–to–Boston shuttle
for what seemed the thousandth time,
I recalled what seemed a poem:

in the time before jets,
when the last shuttle left
LaGuardia at eleven,
I flew home to Logan

on a virtually empty DC-7
and one of the seven other passengers
I recognized as Al Capp.
Later, at a party,

one of those Cambridge parties
where his anti-Ho politics
were wrong, so wrong
the left eventually broke his heart,

I recalled this to him,
but did not recall how sleepy
he looked to me, how tired,
with his peg-legged limp

and rich man's blue suit
and Li'l Abner shock of hair.
He laughed and said to me,
"And if the plane had crashed,

can't you see the headline?—
ONLY EIGHT KILLED.
ONLY EIGHT KILLED: everyone
would be so relieved!"

Now Al is dead, dead,
and the shuttle is always crowded.

EAST HAMPTON–BOSTON BY AIR

for Kurt and Jill

Oh dear,
the plane is so small the baggage
is stuffed into its nose

and under its wings,
like the sacs of a honeybee!
There are six of us, mostly women.

We crowd in, crouching
in our summer denims and shades;
we settle, buckle, inhale. Oh

no, we are aloft! like that,
with just a buzz, and Shelter Island
flattens beneath us, between

the forks of Long Island—the twisty
legs of a dancing man, foreshortened,
his head lost in a tan mist.

The plane is too little!
It rides the waves of air
like a rowboat, of aluminum,

sluing, dropping into the troughs;
it gives out a shuddering frug motion
of its shoulders—one, two!

I sit facing
the ladies I am flying to Boston with,
only one of them my wife

but all of them grimacing,
shutting their eyes with a sigh, resting
forehead on fingertips as in sick prayer.

Eyeballs roll, breasts bounce,
nostril-wings turn pale, and hair
comes sweatily undone;

my wife signals
with mirthless terrified lips that only
I can read, "I hate this."

We tip! tip as a body,
skid above some transmitting antennae,
in Rhode Island it must be,

stuck in the Earth like knitting needles
into a ball of yarn: webbed
by wire stays their eerie points rise.

We are high, but not so high
as not to feel high;
the Earth is too clear beneath us,

under glass that must not be touched,
each highway and house and the sites
of our graves but not yet,

not yet, no! Bright wind
toys with us,
tosses us,

our eyes all meet together
in one gel gaze of fear;
we are closer than in coitus;

the girl beside me,
young and Jewish, murmurs
she was only trying to get to Maine.

And now Boston
is its own blue street-map beneath us;
we can feel in the lurch the pilot

trying to pull in Logan
like a great fish
by the throat of the runway.

What invisible castles
of turbulence rise
from the complacent, safe towers!

What ripples of ecstasy
leap
from the wind-whitened water!

The sea-wall, the side-streaming asphalt:
we are down, shouting out
defiance to our own momentum,

and trundle unbroken
back through the static gates
of life, and halt.

Had that been us, aloft?
Unbuckling, we trade
simpers and caresses of wry glance

in farewell, our terror
still moist on our clothes.
One by one

we crouch toward the open and drop,
dishevelled seatbelts left behind
us like an afterbirth.

ON THE WAY TO DELPHI

Oedipus slew his father near this muddy field
the bus glides by as it glides by many another,
and Helicon is real; the Muses hid and dwelled
on a hill, less than a mountain, that we could climb
if the bus would stop and give us the afternoon.

From these small sites, now overrun by roads and fame,
dim chieftains stalked into the world's fog and grew huge.
Where shepherds sang their mistaken kings, stray factories
mar with cement, smoke, and tile the lean geology
that wants to forget—*has* forgotten—the myths it bred.

We pass stone slopes where houses, low, of stone, blend in
like utterings on the verge of sleep—accretions
scarce distinguishable from scree, on the uphill way
to architecture and law. No men are visible.
All out: Parnassus. The oracle's voice is wild.

ISLAND SUN

When the albums of this century's intermingling
are assembled, I hope a page will show
two sunburned young honeymooners from Woonsocket,
Rhode Island, or an aged duo from Short Hills,
New Jersey (he in green pants, she in pink pleats),
gazing into the teeth of a black steel band
beating away and pealing in full flight
while the tropical moon leans lopsided overhead—

lopsided because its face is tilted differently
at these holiday latitudes, just as the air
yields different constellations, and summer
is not a season to be earned but always there:
outside the louvered door, the vertical sunlight
like a face of childhood, too good to be true.
The steel band wears mismatching tank tops
and speaks an English too liquid to understand.

Ghosts, we flit through a phantasmal summer
we have earned with dollar-shaped months of living
under clouds, in cold cities that are clouds.
We burn. Our noses have been painted red!
For the white transparent fish that flutter
away from our glass masks, the turquoise water
is paradise; but what of the mahogany man
entranced in his shack by the sea-grape tree?

His irises are like licked Lifesavers, so thin.
He smiles to see us rob him of the sun,

the golden pain he has anesthetized with rum.
Let's play that he's invisible. Six days
of sand like sugar, salt baths, and soft nights,
and you have learned to love your body again:
as brown as a stranger beheld in a mirror
whose back is gilded each time the planet turns.

THE MOONS OF JUPITER

Callisto, Ganymede, Europa, Io:
these four, their twinkling spied by Galileo
in his new-invented telescope, debunked
the dogma of celestial spheres—great bubbles
of crystal turning one within the other,
our green and pancake Earth the Edenic center,
and, like a beehive, Purgatory hung below,
and angels scattered all throughout, chiming
and trumpeting across the curved interstices
their glad and constant news. Not so. "*E pur
si muove*," Galileo muttered, *sotto
voce*, having recanted to the Pope.

Yet, it moves, the Earth, and unideal
also the Galilean moons; their motion
and fluctuant occlusions pierced Jove's sphere
and let out all the air that Dante breathed
as tier by singing tier he climbed to where
Beatrice awaited, frosting bride
atop the universal wedding cake.
Not Vergil now but *Voyager*, cloned gawker
sent spinning through symptotic skies
and televising back celestial news,
guides us to the brink of the bearable.

Callisto is the outermost satellite
and the first our phantom footsteps tread.
Its surface underfoot is ancient ice,
thus frozen firm four billion years ago

and chipped and peppered since into a slurry
of saturated cratering. Pocked, knocked,
and rippled sullenly, this is the terrain
of unforgiven wrongs and hurts preserved—
the unjust parental slap, the sneering note
passed hand to hand in elementary school,
the sexual insult confided between cool sheets,
the bad review, the lightly administered snub.
All, in this gloom, keep jagged edges fresh
as yesterday, and, muddied by some silicon,
the bitter spikes and uneroded rims
of ancient impact trip and lacerate
our progress. There is no horizon, just
widespread proof of ego's bombardment.

Next, Ganymede, the largest of these moons,
as large as toasted Mercury. Its ice enchants
with ponds where we can skate and peek down through
pale recent crazings to giant swarthy flakes
of mineral mystery; raked blocks like glaciers
must be traversed, and vales of strange grooves cut
by a parallel sliding, implying
tectonic activity, a once-warmed interior.
This is the realm of counterthrust—the persistent
courtship, the job application, the punch
given back to the ribs of the opposing tackle.
A rigid shame attends these ejecta,
and a grim satisfaction we did not go under
meekly, but thrust our nakedness hard
against the skin of the still-fluid world,
leaving what is called here a ghost crater.

. . .

"Cue ball of the satellites"—so joked
the *National Geographic* of Europa.
But landed on the fact, the mind's eye swims
in something somber and delicious both—
a merged Pacific and Siberia,
an opalescent deadness veined with beige
and the whole suffused by a flickering rose
tint taken from great, rotating Jupiter.
Europa's surface stretches still and smooth,
so smooth its horizon's glossy limb betrays
an arc of curvature. The meteors here
fell on young flesh and left scars
no deeper than birthmarks; as we walk
our chins are lit from underneath, the index
of reflection, the albedo, is so high.
Around us glares the illusion of success:
a certain social polish, decent grades,
accreditations, memberships, applause,
and mutual overlookings melt together
to form one vast acceptance that makes us blind.

On Io, volcanoes plume, and sulfur tugged
by diverse gravitations bubbles forth
from a golden crust that caps a molten sea.
The atmosphere smells foul, and pastel snow
whips burningly upon us, amid the cold.
This is our heart, our bowels, ever renewed,
the poisonous churn of basic needs
suffering the pull of bodies proximate.
The bulblike reptile brain, the mother's breast,
the fear of death, the wish to kill, the itch

to plunge and flee, the love of excrement,
the running sore and appetitive mouth
all find form here. Kilometers away,
a melancholy puckered caldera
erupts, and magma, gas, and crystals hurl
upward in a smooth blue column that
umbrellas overhead—some particles
escaping Io's seething gravity.

Straining upward out of ourselves to follow
their flight, we confront the forgotten
witness, Jupiter's thunderous mass,
the red spot roaring like an anguished eye
amid a turbulence of boiling eyebrows—
an emperor demented but enthroned,
and hogging with his gases an empyrean
in which the Sun is just another star.
So, in a city, as we hurry along
or swiftly ascend to the sixtieth floor,
enormity suddenly dawns and we become
beamwalkers treading a hand's-breadth of steel,
the winds of space shining around our feet.
Striated by slow-motion tumult
and lowering like a cloud, the planet turns,
vast ball, annihilating *other*,
epitome of ocean, mountain, cityscape
whose mass would crush us were we once
to stop the inward chant, *This is not real.*

Seven Odes to Seven
Natural Processes

ODE TO ROT

Der gut Herr Gott
said, "Let there be rot,"
and hence bacteria and fungi sprang
into existence to dissolve the knot
of carbohydrates photosynthesis
achieves in plants, in living plants.
Forget the parasitic smuts,
the rusts, the scabs, the blights, the wilts, the spots,
the mildews and aspergillosis—
the fungi gone amok,
attacking living tissue,
another instance, did Nature need another,
of predatory heartlessness.
Pure rot
is not
but benign; without it, how
would the forest digest its fallen timber,
the woodchuck corpse
vanish to leave behind a poem?
Dead matter else would hold the elements in thrall—
nitrogen, phosphorus, gallium
forever locked into the slot
where once they chemically triggered
the lion's eye, the lily's relaxing leaf.

All sparks dispersed
to that bad memory wherein the dream of life
fails of recall, let rot
proclaim its revolution:

the microscopic hyphae sink
their fangs of enzyme into the rosy peach
and turn its blush a yielding brown,
a mud of melting glucose:
once-staunch committees of chemicals now vote
to join the invading union,
the former monarch and constitution routed
by the riot of rhizoids,
the thalloid consensus.

The world, reshuffled, rolls to renewed fullness;
the oranges forgot
in the refrigerator "produce" drawer
turn green and oblate
and altogether other than edible,
yet loom as planets of bliss to the ants at the dump.
The banana peel tossed from the Volvo
blackens and rises as roadside chicory.
Bodies loathsome with their maggotry of ghosts resolve
to earth and air,
their fire spent, and water there
as a minister must be, to pronounce the words.
All process is reprocessing;
give thanks for gradual ceaseless rot
gnawing gross Creation fine while we sleep,
the lightning-forged organic conspiracy's
merciful counterplot.

TO EVAPORATION

What lifts the ocean into clouds
and dries our ink upon the page?
What gives the porous pavement, an hour after rain,
its sycamore-bark-splotchy steaminess
as molecules of H_2O leap from the fading film
to find lodging in air's loose lattices?
Evaporation,
that random breach of surface tension
by molecules "which happen to acquire exceptionally high
velocities." Brave "happening"!—they fly
the minute distance across
and join another state of matter,
sacrificing, as they depart, heat
to the attraction of the molecules still water,
like a wedlocked beauty leaving behind
her filmy nightgowns as she flees to a better lover.

Fidelity of process!
The housewife trusts
the sheets left out upon the line to dry,
and on Anguilla, where I spent a winter once,
the natives trusted
the great salt pond behind our home to yield
its annual harvest of sublimated salt.
All around us, water is rising
on invisible wings
to fall as dew, as rain, as sleet, as snow,
while overhead the nested giant domes
of atmospheric layers roll

and in their revolutions lift
humidity north and south
from the equator toward the frigid, arid poles,
where latitudes become mere circles.
Molecular to global, the kinetic order rules
unseen and omnipresent,
merciful and laughingly subtle like the breathing of naiads.
The ladies of Anguilla, lilting in their kerchiefs,
with pale-nailed black hands would spread
their festive damp wash
on the bushes around their shacks to dry,
the scents of skin and soap and oleander confounded
in this process as elemental
as the rain showers that would fall so quickly
sun, caught shining,
made of each hurtling drop a spear of fire.

As a child I—
I,
the tiniest of nominatives, the atom that "happens"—
watched the blood dry on my wounds
and observed how a cup of spilled water
would certainly vanish
with no more cause than time,
leaving behind as stain
only the dust its tumble of molecules had gathered
or, if the cup had been sweet, the sugar
left faintly behind as precipitate.
Trivial matters!
But I exulted
in the sensation of delivery,
of vapor carrying skyward, just as gravity

hurled water, twisting, down the sink and scummed gutter;
these processes
transpiring without my guilt or willing
were pure pleasure:
unseeable wheels interlocking beyond
all blame and duty and self-exertion,
evaporation
as delicate as mist,
more mighty than a waterfall.

ODE TO GROWTH

Like an awl-tip breaking ice
the green shoot cleaves the gray spring air.
The young boy finds his school-pants cuffs
too high above his shoes when fall returns.
The pencilled marks on the bathroom doorframe climb.
The cells rereplicate,
somatotrophin
comes bubbling down the bloodstream, a busybody
with instructions for the fingernails,
another set for the epiderm,
a third for the budding mammae,
all hot from the hypothalamus
and admitting of no editing,
lest dwarves result, or cretins, or neoplasms.
In spineless crustaceans
the machinery of molting is controlled
by phasing signals from nervous ganglia
located, often, in the eyestalks, where these exist.
In plants
a family of auxins,
shuttling up and down,
inhibit or encourage cell elongation
as eventual shapeliness demands,
and veto lateral budding while apical growth proceeds,
and even determine abscission—
the falling of leaves.
For death and surrender
are part of growth's package.

· · ·

"It's just the eye's way of growing,"
my ophthalmologist euphemizes
of the lens's slow stiffening
and irreversible presbyopia.
Skin goes keratinous,
the epiphyses of the long bones unite with the shaft,
and "linear growth comes to an end."
Comes to an end!
Our aging's a mystery, as is our sleep:
the protein codes, transactions more elaborate
than the accounts of a thousand dummy trusts,
have their smuggling secrets still.

The meanwhile, let us die
rejoicing,
as around us uncountable husks
are split and shed by the jungle push of green
and the swell of fresh bone
echoes the engendering tumescence.
Time's line being a one-way street,
we must walk the tight rope or fly.
Growth is life's lockstep;
we shall never again sit next to Peggy Lutz
in third grade, her breasts
a mere glint on the curve of her tomboy vigor
and our whiskery doom
within us of less dimension than a freckle.

TO FRAGMENTATION

Motion, motion.
Within the body cells
each nucleus rotates widdershins
and mitochondria hustle round and round.
All things move, even the continents and Polaris,
those epitomes of stability.
Sun and gravity
push and pull.
Moisture seeps, and night-frost splits.
Glaciers rub a sandpaper of boulders
down U-shaped valleys,
and tectonic uplift
in slow motion shatters the friable shelves of shale.
Carbon dioxide is washed from the air
or the roots of plants:
the resultant carbonic acid
pries loose the glittering grip of flint upon flint.
Dampness evaporates
rapidly from the skin of stone but lingers within,
transforming granite into clay,
which swells,
spalling loose thin flakes like bark from a rotting tree.

At the cliff's base builds a slope of scree.
At the ocean's edge
the waves in a Shakespearean tumult pummel with pebbles
gripped in the fingers of their froth
the shore;
their millennial frenzy carves

the dizzying gills
and the stacks of stratified sediment
we marvelled at, visiting Caithness.
Remember, Martha?
The grass-bearing, cow-feeding turf
worn by those cliffs like a debonair cape?

Breaking, breaking,
eaten, eaten,
the mother rock yields her sands and silts,
each grain of sand a monolith,
each Matterhorn a heap of potential till.
"The eternal mountains were scattered,
the everlasting hills sank low."
The pompous rivers conduct their symphonies of erosion,
and the mites in the subterrene dark
mince finer their mineral meal.
No, nothing is "too, too solid."
All things mundane must slide and weather.
Heat and cold saw back and forth,
and wet and dry;
wind and water and ice and life
have powdered our planet's obdurate skin.
But
had not Earth's aboriginal rock
submitted to fragmentation's lash,
no regolith would have seasoned into soil,
and the imaginary
would never have taken root.

ODE TO ENTROPY

Some day—can it be believed?—
in the year 10^{70} or so,
single electrons and positrons will orbit
one another to form atoms bonded
across regions of space
greater than the present observable universe.
"Heat death" will prevail.
The stars long since will have burnt their hydrogen
and turned to iron.
Even the black holes will have decayed.
Entropy!
thou seal on extinction,
thou curse on Creation.
All change distributes energy,
spills what cannot be gathered again.
Each meal, each smile,
each foot-race to the well by Jack and Jill
scatters treasure, lets fall
gold straws once woven from the resurgent dust.
The night sky blazes with Byzantine waste.
The bird's throbbling is expenditure,
and the tide's soughing,
and the tungsten filament illumining my hand.

A ramp has been built into probability
the universe cannot re-ascend.
For our small span,
the sun has fuel, the moon lifts the lulling sea,
the highway shudders with stolen hydrocarbons.

How measure these inequalities
so massive and luminous
in which one's self is secreted
like a jewel mislaid in mountains of garbage?
Or like that bright infant Prince William,
with his whorled nostrils and blank blue eyes,
to whom empire and all its estates are already assigned.
Does its final diffusion
deny a miracle?
Those future voids are scrims of the mind,
pedagogic as blackboards.

Did you know
that four-fifths of the body's intake goes merely
to maintain our temperature of 98.6°?
Or that Karl Barth, addressing prisoners, said
the prayer for stronger faith is the one prayer
that has never been denied?
Death exists nowhere in nature, not
in the minds of birds or the consciousness of flowers,
not even in the numb brain of the wildebeest calf
gone under to the grinning crocodile, nowhere
in the mesh of woods or the tons of sea, only
in our forebodings, our formulae.
There is still enough energy in one overlooked star
to power all the heavens madmen have ever proposed.

TO CRYSTALLIZATION

The atom is a crystal
of a sort; the lattices
its interlockings form
lend a planarity most pleasing
to the abysses and cliffs, much magnified,
of (for example) salt and tourmaline.
Arise, order,
out of necessity!
Mock, you crystals,
with all appearance of chiselled design,
our hope of a Grand Artificer.
The graceful layered frost-ferns the midnight elves
left on the Shillington windowpanes
for my morning astonishment were misinformation,
as is
the glittering explosion of tinted quartz
discovered in earth like a heart of thought,
buried evidence
crying out for release to the workman's pick,
tangled hexagonal hair of an angel interred
where it fell, our earth still molten, in the Fall.

When, on those anvils at the center of stars
and those even more furious anvils
of the exploding supernovae,
the heavy elements were beaten together
to the atomic number of 94
and the crystalline metals with their easily lost
valence electrons arose,

their malleability and conductivity
made Assyrian goldsmithing possible,
and most of New York City.

Stendhal thought that love
should be likened to a bare branch crystallized
by a winter in the depths of the salt mines of Hallein:
"the tiniest twigs, no bigger
than a tomtit's claws, are spangled with an infinite
number of shimmering, glistening crystals."
Our mathematics and hope of Heaven
alike look to crystals;
their arising, the mounting
of molecules one upon the other, suggests
that inner freezing whereby inchoate
innocence compresses a phrase of art.
Music rises in its fixed lattices
and its cries of aspiration chill our veins
with snowflakes of blood;
the mind grapples up an inflexible relation
and the stiff spheres chime—
themselves, the ancients thought, all crystal.
In this seethe of hot muck there is *something else*:
the ribs of an old dory emerge from the sand,
the words set their bevelled bite on the page,
the loved one's pale iris flares in silent assent,
the electrons leap, leaving positive ions
as the fish-scales of moonlight show us water's perfect dance.
Steno's Law, crystallography's first:
the form of crystal admits no angle but its own.

ODE TO HEALING

A scab
is a beautiful thing—a coin
the body has minted, with an invisible motto:
In God We Trust.
Our body loves us,
and, even while the spirit drifts dreaming,
works at mending the damage that we do.
That heedless Ahab the conscious mind
drives our thin-skinned hull onto the shoals;
a million brilliant microscopic engineers below
shore up the wound with platelets,
lay down the hardening threads of fibrin,
send in the lymphocytes, and supervise
those cheery swabs, the macrophages, in their clean-up.
Break a bone, and fibroblasts
knit tight the blastema in days.
Catch a cold, and the fervid armies
swarm to blanket our discomfort in sleep.
For all these centuries of fairy tales poor men
butchered each other in the name of cure,
not knowing an iota of what the mute brute body knew.

Logically, benevolence surrounds us.
In fire or ice, we would not be born.
Soft tissue bespeaks a soft world.
Yet, can it have been malevolence
that taught the skinned knuckle to heal
or set the white scar on my daughter's glossy temple?

Besieged, we are supplied,
from caustic saliva down,
with armaments against the hordes,
"the slings and arrows," "the thousand natural shocks."

Not quite benevolence.
Not quite its opposite.
A perfectionism, it would almost seem,
stuck with matter's recalcitrance,
as, in the realm of our behavior, with
the paradox of freedom.
Well, can we add a cubit to our height
or heal ourselves by taking conscious thought?
The spirit sits as a bird singing
high in a grove of hollow trees whose red sap rises
saturated with advice.
To the child as he scuffles up an existence
out of pebbles and twigs
and finds that even paper cuts, and games can hurt,
the small assemblage of a scab
is like the slow days' blurring of a deep disgrace,
the sinking of a scolding into time.
Time heals: not so;
time is the context of forgetting and of remedy
as aseptic phlegms
lave the scorched membranes,
the capillaries and insulted nerves.
Close your eyes, knowing
that healing is a work of darkness,
that darkness is a gown of healing,
that the vessel of our tremulous venture is lifted

by tides we do not control.
Faith is health's requisite:
we have this fact in lieu
of better proof of *le bon Dieu*.

Light Verse

THE ROCKETTES

Now when those girls, all thirty-six, go
to make their silky line, they do it slow,
so slow and with a smile—they know
we love it, we the audience. Our
breaths suck in with a gasp you hear
as their legs in casual unison
wave this way then, and that, and their top
hats tilt in one direction,
and their sharp feet twinkle like a starry row
as the pace accelerates, and the lazy legs
(thirty-six, thirty-six, what a sex
to be limber and white and slender
and fat all at once, all at once!)
that seemed so calm go higher, higher
in the wonderful kicks, like the teeth
of a beast we have dreamed and are dreaming,
like the feathers all velvet together
of a violent contracting that pulls us in,
then lets us go, that pulls us in,
then lets us go; they smile because
they know we know they know we know.

DEA EX MACHINA

In brief, shapeliness and smoothness of the flesh are
desirable because they are signs of biological efficiency.
—David Angus, *The New York Times Book Review*

My love is like Mies van der Rohe's
    "Machine for living"; she,
Divested of her underclothes,
    Suggests efficiency.

Her supple shoulders call to mind
    A set of bevelled gears;
Her lower jaw has been aligned
    To hinge behind her ears.

Her hips, sweet ball-and-socket joints,
    Are padded to perfection;
Each knee, with its patella, points
    In just the right direction.

Her fingertips remind me of
    A digital computer;
She simply couldn't be, my love,
    A millimeter cuter.

YOUNG MATRONS DANCING

Corinna foots it in bare feet;
Her toes are dusty but discreet
In sliding backwards from the shoes
Of Arthur Johnson Betelgeuse.

Anthea, married twice with three
Small children, softly smiles to see
Her jealous present husband frown
While talking stocks with Hubert Brown.

These pelves childbirth spread still twitch
In time to that too-narrow itch
That led their innocence down ways
Composed of endless working days;

Corinna and Anthea still
Can bend to Lester Lanin's will,
And mime with scarce-diminished grace
Perpetuation of the race.

SHAVING MIRROR

Among the Brobdingnagians Gulliver
complained of the pores, the follicles,
"with a mole here and there as broad as a trencher,
and hairs hanging from it thicker than pack-threads."

Swift hated everything's being so relative,
"so varified with spots, pimples, and freckles
that nothing could appear more nauseous";
but hell, here we are, bad clay.

In this polished concavity mute enlargement
hovers on my skin like a flea-sized plane
surveying another earth, some solemn planet
hung long in space unknown, a furtive star.

Draw closer, visitor; these teeth
trumpet their craters, my lips are shores,
my eyes bloody lakes, the lashes alarming,
my whiskers like leafless trees—there is life!

"But the most hateful sight of all was the lice
crawling on their clothes"—an image echoed
by the King, who pronounces that men must "be
the most pernicious race of little odious

vermin that nature ever suffered to crawl
upon the surface of the earth." Hard words
from above. I say, the more there is
of me, the more there is to love.

Beyond all reproach, beyond readjustment,
among the corruptible heavenly bodies
I swim, eluding my measure, "my complexion
made up of several colors altogether disagreeable."

FOOD

It is always there,
Man's *real* best friend.
It never bites back;
it is already dead.
It never tells us we are lousy lovers
or asks us for an interview.
It simply begs, *Take me;*
it cries out, *I'm yours.*
Mush me all up, it says;
Whatever is you, is pure.

SELF-SERVICE

Always I wanted to do it myself
and envied the oily-handed boy
paid by the station to lift
the gun from its tall tin holster
and squeeze. That was power,
hi-octane or lo-, and now no-lead.

What feminism has done for some sisters
self-service has done for me.
The pulsing hose is mine, the numbers
race—the cents, the liquid tenths—
according to my pressure, mine!
I squeeze. This is power:

transparent horsepower, blood
of the sands, bane of the dollar,
soul-stuff; the nozzle might jump
from my grip, it appears to tremble
through its fumes. Myself,
I pinch off my share, and pay.

ENERGY: A VILLANELLE

The logs give back, in burning, solar fire
   green leaves imbibed and processed one by one;
nothing is lost but, still, the cost grows higher.

The ocean's tons of tide, to turn, require
   no more than time and moon; it's cosmic fun.
The logs give back, in burning, solar fire.

All microörganisms must expire
   and quite a few became petroleum;
nothing is lost but, still, the cost grows higher.

The oil rigs in Bahrain imply a buyer
   who counts no cost, when all is said and done.
The logs give back, in burning, solar fire

but Good Gulf gives it faster; every tire
   is by the fiery heavens lightly spun.
Nothing is lost but, still, the cost grows higher.

So guzzle gas, the leaden night draws nigher
   when cinders mark where stood the blazing sun.
The logs give back, in burning, solar fire;
nothing is lost but, still, the cost grows higher.

TYPICAL OPTICAL

In the days of my youth
   'Mid many a caper
I drew with my nose
   A mere inch from the paper;
But now that I'm older
   And of the elite
I find I can't focus
   Inside of two feet.

First pill-bottle labels
   And telephone books
Began to go under
   To my dirty looks;
Then want ads and box scores
   Succumbed to the plague
Of the bafflingly quite
   Unresolvably vague.

Now novels and poems
   By Proust and John Donne
Recede from my ken in
   Their eight-point Granjon;
Long, long in the lens
   My old eyeballs enfold
No print any finer
   Than sans-serif **bold.**

ON THE RECENTLY MINTED
HUNDRED-CENT PIECE

as of 1979

What have they done to our dollar, darling,
    And who is this Susan B.
Anthony in her tight collar, darling,
    Instead of Miss Liberty?

Why seems it the size of a quarter, dearie,
    Why is it infernally small?
To fit in the palm of a porter, dearie,
    As tip, though he mutter, "That's all?"

Who shrank it, our greenback and buck, beloved,
    And made it a plaything of tin?
Father Time, Uncle Sam, Lady Luck, beloved,
    Have done done our doll dollar in.

LIGHT-HEADED IN SWEDEN

for Bertil Käll

I.

The trams in Amsterdam are yellow
  Or gray; in Oslo, blue.
In Copenhagen, bisexuals bicycle
  And take the buses, too.
In Stockholm, by serene canals
  Big-bellied hotels float;
If you want to go to the Archipelago,
  You'd better take a båt.

II.

There was a young student of Lund
Whose -erstanding was not always und;
  "But up in Uppsala,"
  He said, "*every schola*
Is as dumb as the fish in the Sund!"

THE LAMENT OF
ABRASHKA TERTZ

*(A Translation of a Russian Song,
with the Help of Andrew Field)*

All Moscow knows the loving pair we call
   Sonka-the-Snatch and snatch-purse Abram Tertz.*
He's rummaged in the pockets of us all,
   And all in turn have rummaged round in hers.

Now one day Abram stumbled on a stake—
   Don't ask me how, the rubles just arrived—
And, moved to tears, he threw himself a wake
   For all the lousy years he had survived.

He bought some herring and, so they could swim,
   A river's worth of hooch. Time gurgled by,
A guest commenced to strum, and Abraham
   Began to wring a concertina dry.

Old "On the Moldavanka" was the song.
   Sweet Sonka, having downed a goodly bowl,
Was laid out stoned; her lover drew a long
   Wet breath and thusly vomited his soul:

---

* The pen name of the dissident Soviet writer Andrei Sinyavski,
whose trial in early 1966 quickened Western interest in this folk
song from the last years of Stalin's labor camps; such songs en-
joyed a vogue among Moscow intellectuals in the late Fifties, when
Sinyavski began to write.

"Go screw you, Sonka, with your pretty airs.
    Your bed is full of lice, and I was one.
I talked to Squint, and in his cups he swears
    You've slept with every Russian mother's son!

"The whole street knows, and everybody laughs;
    I can't walk down the sidewalk any more.
The scum, they clap and wink when I go past—
    And all because of you, you stinking whore!"

THE VISIONS OF
MACKENZIE KING

*(Based, More Closely Than You Might Think,
Upon Articles in the Toronto* Globe and Mail*)*

I, William Lyon Mackenzie King,
age seventy-three in 1948,
Prime Minister of Canada for twenty-two years,
had visions, and as such recorded them,
though merer men might call them dreams.

In one I saw Hitler
sewing buttons on a bed quilt.
My interpretation: "a lesson in patience."

In another, Franklin Roosevelt
and I were in the home of a wealthy man,
unnamed. As we speculated
upon the means (suspect, somehow)
whereby our host had acquired his fortune,
I had to sit awkwardly upon the floor.
The meaning was clear: I should return
to "some simpler life."

In yet another, the then Princess
Juliana of the Netherlands
and her charming consort, Prince Bernhard,
came up to me ceremoniously;
I looked down and discovered

I was wearing an old-fashioned nightgown!
And, later in the dream, lacked trousers.
But no interpretation
was confided to my journal.

Mr. and Mrs. Winston Churchill
were at Laurier House, my guests; in my unease
I felt things amiss, and hastened
to offer the great man a drink and a cigar.
He had already helped himself to both.
My valet took a swig from the decanter
and in my rage I hit the presuming fellow
with a felt hat that had appeared in my hand.

I climbed a tower. There was room at the top.
But my valet, Nicol, informed me
a "private woman's club" had occupied the premises
and there could be no admission for me.
My conclusion: the summit of my calling
had been reached, but once there
I would not find the society of women
nor "what I had striven for most."

I, W. L. Mackenzie King,
recorded these visions now released
some thirty years later, as a species
of Canadian history. Now,
as then, I am embarrassed. Among
French dignitaries, my nose began to bleed.
My handkerchief was stained with blood!
"I tried to keep it discreetly out of sight."
Next, in a shadowy warehouse setting,

"furies" endeavored to assassinate me.
When I awoke at last, Gandhi was dead.

The world's blood pursued me. The great
ignored my *gaffes*. But truth will out.
The newspapers titter, I was insecure.
Shaving soap spoke to me, of Mother and dogs,
in those decades of demons of whom I was one.

A NOTE ABOUT THE AUTHOR

JOHN UPDIKE *was born in 1932, in Shillington, Pennsylvania. He graduated from Harvard College in 1954 and spent a year as a Knox Fellow at the Ruskin School of Drawing and Fine Art in Oxford, England. From 1955 to 1957 he was a staff member of* The New Yorker, *to which he has contributed short stories, poems, and book reviews. He is the author of eleven novels and fifteen or so other books, including four collections of verse. Since 1957, he has lived in Massachusetts.*

A NOTE ON THE TYPE

The text of this book was set on the Linotype in Janson, a recutting made directly from type cast from matrices long thought to have been made by the Dutchman Anton Janson, who was a practicing type founder in Leipzig during the years 1668–87. However, it has been conclusively demonstrated that these types are actually the work of Nicholas Kis (1650–1702), a Hungarian, who most probably learned his trade from the Dutch type founder Dirk Voskens. The type is an excellent example of the influential and sturdy Dutch types that prevailed in England up to the time William Caslon developed his own incomparable designs from them.

Composed by Maryland Linotype Composition Company, Inc.
Baltimore, Maryland

Printed and bound by The Haddon Craftsmen, Inc.
Scranton, Pennsylvania